THE HIGH-IMPACT SALES MANAGER

A No-Nonsense, Practical Guide to Improve Your Team's Sales Performance

NORMAN BEHAR

DAVID JACOBY

RAY MAKELA

The skills, techniques and models shared in this book are based on proven methodologies and practices employed by Sales Readiness Group (SRG) to help clients improve sales performance. With this in mind, we thank the entire SRG Team for their ongoing commitment to developing and implementing industry leading sales and sales management training programs.

Contents

Foreword 1

Introduction: Transcending the Daily Grind 5

Section 1: Sales Management Challenges 9

Where Do Great Sales Managers Come From? 11

Sales Management Time Trap 13

Section 2: Building A Great Team 15

Developing a Job Profile 18

Sourcing Candidates 23

Screen Resumes 25

Conduct Phone Interviews 26

In-Person Interviews 29

Selecting the Right Candidate 32

Section 3: Managing Your Team 35

Behavior-Based Performance Management 37

Communicating Expectations 41

Managing Performance Gains and Gaps 44

Performance Counseling 49

Section 4:   Managing the Sales Pipeline 57

Avoiding a Bloated Pipeline 60

The Relationship between Sales Process and Pipeline 62

Three Steps to Improve Forecast Accuracy 63

Section 5:   Coaching Your Team 69

Sales Coaching Mindset 71

Two Types of Coaching 75

Co-Assessment 85

Three Types of Calls 86

Five-Step Process for Sales Coaching 88

Managing Resistance to Coaching 96

Are You a Good Coach? 101

Section 6:   Leading Your Team 105

Developing and Achieving Your Sales Vision 107

How to Make Important Decisions 112

How to Influence Your Team 116

Six Common Motives of Salespeople 120

Confidence in Your Team.............................124

Transforming Into a High-Impact Sales Leader.......127

Appendices...131

A: Candidate Selection Tool 133

B: Sales Performance Causes/Action Flowchart 135

C: Sales Coaching Plan 137

D: Coaching Call Observation Form 139

E: VisiPlan Tool 141

Glossary.. 143

About the Authors 147

Norman Behar.. 147

David Jacoby.. 148

Ray Makela 149

About Sales Readiness Group 151

Foreword

In 40 years, I've seen a lot of change in the sales profession. From technology tools, to social media, to mobile devices, we're surrounded by solutions that promise to make salespeople and managers more productive and effective.

Ironically, however, these elements have not necessarily made it easier for sales managers to figure out how to master their craft. On the contrary, we are producing a generation of sales leaders who are rich in technology but have little to no idea of how to properly build, grow, and manage their teams. The art of sales management remains elusive.

Poor sales management is a real liability. In fact, the effectiveness of frontline sales managers directly correlates to a company's capacity to increase revenue and post consistent profits. That's because sales managers do the hard work that greases the wheels of success. This includes hiring the right people, producing accurate forecasts, coaching middle performers to close more deals, and leading their teams to success. These are all basic building blocks of a high-performance team.

The principals at Sales Readiness Group understand this inside and out. They have spent more than 20 years helping sales managers create elite sales teams. Their insight regularly helps sales managers achieve the necessary perspective to realize short- and long-term goals, learn vital management skills, and avoid common pitfalls. In short, they help sales managers get the kind of results that keep companies on the path to profitable growth for years to come.

That's why I'm excited that the principals of Sales Readiness Group have taken the time to write this book. *The High-Impact Sales Manager* will give any practitioner a comprehensive framework for sales management success in the key areas of hiring, coaching, performance management, motivation and leadership. For anyone who wants to achieve increased levels of success in sales management, this book should be on your required reading list.

At the end of the day, everyone in a sales organization has a desire to be successful. Salespeople want to compete to beat quota and win recognition and rewards. Sales managers want to make sales productivity and performance soar. CEOs want to see record-breaking profits. The key to fulfilling these goals does not lie solely in the newest devices or technology tools. It also lies in the simple habit of taking a step back from the daily grind to seek new insight and wisdom. With that in mind, I wish you great success as you learn and apply the skills and techniques from *The High-Impact Sales Manager.*

Gerhard Gschwandtner

Founder and publisher

Selling Power magazine

Transcending
the Daily Grind

The sales manager's job is one of the most challenging in a sales organization. Performance metrics are visible to the entire organization, management pressure to "hit the numbers" is intense, and the pace of managing a sales team can be overwhelming. Many sales managers find that they spend much of their time putting out fires, and moving from problem to problem. Their days consist of an overwhelming number of activities including responding to urgent requests from their bosses, resolving customer issues and complaints, and dealing with disgruntled employees.

In addition, they find themselves sitting in meetings that go on too long, and submitting countless sales forecasts to satisfy upper management. As a result, sales managers get caught up in a daily grind and end their workweek exhausted and feeling like they have little control over their destiny. They are also frustrated knowing that the cycle will repeat itself the following Monday. The toll on the sales manager is significant and can also leave his or her salespeople feeling rudderless.

But it doesn't have to be this way. Based on our experience leading, coaching, and training sales teams, we have developed a simple and powerful program that includes the systems, processes, skills, and techniques to allow you to become a High-Impact Sales Manager.

The High-Impact Sales Manager transcends the daily grind and is both confident and enthusiastic, knowing he or she is leading and empowering the team to achieve unparalleled success.

In the following sections you will learn how to overcome these challenges, hire the best people, manage sales performance, produce accurate sales forecasts, provide coaching that drives performance, and lead your team to greatness.

Sales Management
Challenges

Where Do Great Sales Managers Come From?

Managing a sales team is one of the most important and demanding positions in a company, and it requires a unique set of skills. Unfortunately, if you're like most sales managers, you started your sales management career ill equipped to effectively manage a team of salespeople based on your prior sales experience. This is what we call the "Star Athlete" Syndrome, and it plagues most sales organizations.

In any team sport, we can find great examples of star athletes who transitioned from player to coach, but failed miserably. The skills that made them great athletes didn't automatically allow them to become a great coach or manager – success in these areas required a different skillset. This isn't to say that it's impossible for a great athlete to make a great coach, but we shouldn't assume it will happen just because he or she is a great individual player.

Here's how the Star Athlete Syndrome happens in a sales organization. A star salesperson grows tired of the daily grind of being an individual contributor and aspires to move up within the organization. Meanwhile, the vice president of sales is under pressure to fill a vacant sales manager position. The vice president assumes that the star salesperson will naturally be able to translate his or her success as a sales professional to the people he or she will manage.

The reality is that most top-performing salespeople struggle to successfully make the transition from being an individual contributor to manager. That's because star salespeople achieve results on their own, whereas great managers achieve results through the performance of others.

As noted in the table below, the skills that a salesperson needs to master to achieve individual success are very different from the skills you'll need to achieve success through your team.

Salesperson	Sales Manager
Prospecting skills	Setting team goals, priorities
Questioning skills	Recruiting & hiring
Listening/communication	Coaching
Managing objections	Sales performance management
Gaining commitment	Leadership & motivation
Time management (self)	Time management (team)
Product knowledge	Industry knowledge and trends

Figure 1.1: Salesperson vs Sales Manager Skills

Most salespeople respect a manager who's walked in their shoes, and this respect can be a great leadership asset for you. However, the key driver of your long-term success is not only credibility, but also mastery of a specific set of sales-management skills. In order to produce exceptional sales results from the team, you must:

- Build a team of great sales professionals with the requisite attributes to succeed.

- Manage sales performance by focusing on the underlying behaviors that drive sales results.

- Manage the sales pipeline to ensure that opportunities are active and progressing.

- Provide ongoing sales coaching to help salespeople develop their full potential.

- Lead and motivate your team.

Sales Management Time Trap

The transition from salesperson to sales manager includes a number of totally new challenges and time constraints. On a daily basis, you'll be faced with:

- Preparing sales forecasts for upper-level managers.

- Attending management meetings.

- Resolving customer issues.

- Dealing with personnel problems.

- Keeping up with administrative duties and Human Resources requirements.

- Responding to urgent requests from executive leadership.

- Handling numerous additional demands depending on the size, complexity, and maturity of your organization.

These are not small tasks, and they often lead to what we call the "sales management time trap." The time trap is being stuck between doing urgent tasks such as closing deals and handling customer issues, while still managing, coaching, and leading your sales team. The number-one complaint we hear from sales managers is that they don't have enough time.

That's usually because they're still stuck in the mindset of an individual contributor, focused on sales activities, as opposed to adopting a sales management mindset focused on how they can best achieve results through their sales team.

Building a
Great Team

The task of building a great sales team puts many new managers on unfamiliar footing. Not only are they figuring out how to manage a stable of existing salespeople, they must now find ways to recruit, hire, and retain new ones.

Great teams are only as good as their players. So your first job is to understand that building a strong team starts with developing a deep pool of potential candidates and making wise hiring decisions.

Over the years, we've developed the following process for finding and hiring the best possible salespeople for your organization. Here are the steps we'll review.

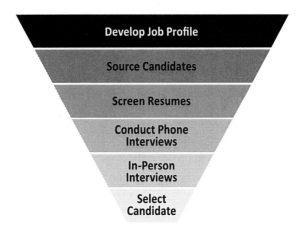

Figure 2.1: Hiring Funnel

The Pitfalls of a Bad Hire

It's easy to fall victim to a few mistakes when it comes to hiring. One, you hire too quickly because you feel pressure to fill the position sooner rather than later. Two, you rely on instinct to find a good fit, rather than use a systematic process.

Both of these actions often lead to making bad hires and this causes bigger problems. Not only are you still losing the revenue you hoped to gain by filling the position, you've lost time and money (your own and your company's) in finding, selecting, onboarding, and training this new salesperson. The wrong hire can even damage customer relationships. Some customers see frequent turnover as a red flag and might think about exploring options with a competitor. Other times, customers can become frustrated by frequent changes or simply working with a salesperson who fails to represent your company's standards for service.

Developing a Job Profile

Many sales managers use job descriptions (which are frequently inherited from a predecessor) to guide their hiring decisions. A job description is useful, but only to a point. Typically it defines the responsibilities and expectations associated with a particular position.

However, it usually doesn't take into account the attributes of someone who would do a great job fulfilling those responsibilities and expectations. To assess and screen candidates effectively, you must first create a job profile by identifying the attributes of your top performers.

Each sales organization is different; therefore, the attributes you're looking for will be unique. However, there are five basic criteria you can use to structure your job profile. They are listed below, along with related attributes.

Job Profile Criteria and Attributes

1. Work Experience
   a. Stable job history
   b. Previous sales experience
   c. History of success
2. Prior Performance
   a. Direct responsibility for performance
   b. Track record of results
   c. Career advancement
   d. Achievement in non-work-related activities

3. Skills (Select up to five that are most important for success in your sales organization)
   a. Communication
   b. Business acumen
   c. Prospecting
   d. Building relationships
   e. Call planning
   f. Questioning skills (to identify customer needs)
   g. Presentation skills
   h. Overcoming objections
   i. Negotiating
   j. Gaining commitment

4. Personal Qualities (Select up to three that are most important for success in your sales organization)
   a. Competitive
   b. Motivated
   c. Positive attitude
   d. Resilient (can handle rejection)
   e. Strong work ethic
   f. Judgement
   g. Integrity

5. Education
   a. Preferred level of formal education
   b. Acceptable grade average
   c. Extracurricular activities
   d. Additional training and educational programs

You want to develop the job profile well in advance of starting the hiring process. If you don't take this step, you're more likely to hire based on gut instinct. In almost all cases, your gut will cause you to lean toward the candidate you see as the most likeable. Likeability is a valuable trait, but it's not the sole predictor of success in a sales role.

Creating a List of Desired Skills & Personal Qualities

It is helpful to create a prioritized list of Skills and Personal Qualities. This will help you focus on candidates who possess the attributes necessary to succeed in your organization. During the hiring process, sales managers need to be aware that the attributes they identify as Skills are trainable, whereas the attributes under Personal Qualities are not. Bear this distinction in mind when evaluating candidates. For example, someone who is resilient and has a strong work ethic may have more potential than a candidate who lacks resilience but shows strong aptitude in the desired skills.

You want to create your own criteria based on the attributes that are (or aren't) present in your top performers. The idea is to challenge your current thinking about any assumptions you may have about star performers to see if a new profile emerges.

For instance, you may assume that your candidates must have industry experience—and that may well be true. But, scanning the star performers on your team, are there individuals who came to you without industry experience and were able to get up to speed quickly? If so, maybe you are holding a notion that is outdated and artificially limiting your pool of candidates.

Your job profile has two benefits. One, it allows you to better evaluate candidates relative to each other. Two, it allows you to manage the entire hiring process sensibly and effectively, especially in the later stages. In almost all cases, sales managers will have to submit candidates to their own manager and/or the Human Resources team for review before extending a job offer. If you do your homework to outline the criteria for selection, the Human Resources team will get a better idea of how you narrowed down your selection and how you evaluated each candidate.

The best candidates will possess many of the attributes you're looking for, but rarely will anyone have all of them. It's important not to skip this step because clearly identifying these attributes on the job profile will help you screen resumes and conduct successful interviews—even if you think you already know what attributes your top salespeople possess.

Sourcing Candidates

As a manager, you need to be in constant recruitment mode. Consider college football coaches, who spend nearly as much time recruiting new players as coaching. That's because they understand they'll have a much easier time coaching if they first identify the right talent.

There are two major drivers of hiring: growth and turnover. Success in existing markets, expansion into new markets, and new offerings are typically the biggest influencers of headcount growth and are often factored into business planning. In this case, sales managers have the luxury of being able to plan ahead to add salespeople.

Turnover is usually high in sales organizations, which means you may lose one of your salespeople at any time. If you have 15 to 20 percent turnover and a 10-person team, you can expect to replace one to two salespeople per year.

If you wait until you have a vacancy to fill before looking for candidates, you're already vulnerable to making a poor hiring decision simply because you'll feel pressured to fill the position. Instead, you should always keep an eye out for your next great hire.

If you do your homework and prepare a solid list of contacts and resources, you'll be in a much stronger position whenever one of your existing salespeople leaves the company. Here are four ways you can build a strong network of high-quality potential candidates.

1. Develop new contacts whenever you attend industry events and trade shows.

2. Use customers, suppliers, and professionals within your own organization as referral sources.

3. Develop your connections (customers, partners, colleagues...) on LinkedIn by participating in discussion groups.

4. Use LinkedIn to source candidates. (See below for a sample job announcement.)

Sample Job Announcement for LinkedIn

Hi – We're looking for an exceptional salesperson to work as part of a dynamic, growing team. Candidates must be experienced, motivated, and have a passion for delivering quality results. If you are that person or know someone who may be interested, please contact us. [Insert link to job description here.]

Sourcing candidates is all about building a deep pool of contacts. Over time, your network can become a primary source for generating interest in your job opening. Your contacts might refer you to other great candidates or express a personal interest in applying for the job. (Remember, just because talented salespeople aren't actively seeking new jobs doesn't mean they wouldn't consider making a change if the right opportunity came along.)

Let's go through the numbers and see how many applicants you'll need to consider to hire one great salesperson.

To get three to five qualified candidates, you will typically need 15-20 interested applicants in your recruiting pipeline. You can quickly screen these interested applicants during phone interviews and come up with three to five qualified applicants. We recommend interviewing at least three qualified applicants (in person) for each open position. More would be better, but that may not be realistic if you need to move quickly.

Screen Resumes

When you're in active recruiting mode and start to receive resumes, you want to screen them with your job profile in mind. The purpose of the resume screen is to remove unqualified applicants and include as many as you can into the next step (which is your phone interview). *Note: In many organizations the resume screen (and other recruiting functions) may be performed by Human Resources.*

How can you speed up the resume screening process? In addition to eliminating unqualified candidates, look for red flags. These could include any of the following:

- Gaps in information. This could raise questions about integrity or "hidden facts."

- Poor-quality resumes. This can indicate lack of interest, drive, perseverance, and even questionable work habits.

- Job-hopping (i.e., four or more jobs in four years). This can show impatience, underperformance or lack of direction.

- Too long (i.e., more than three years) in the same position (without any demonstrated growth). This may imply complacency, lack of drive, high comfort level, and difficulty making successful change.

Conduct Phone Interviews

After you've screened resumes, you're ready to set up phone interviews. These should be limited to no more than 15 minutes per candidate. This is simply a quick conversation to see if you are interested in conducting a more in-depth interview with this candidate.

With that in mind, clearly articulate the time frame to the candidate at the beginning of the call. You can say something like, "This is a preliminary conversation so I can get to know a bit more about you, and this will only take about 10 - 15 minutes of your time."

Occasionally you'll think of follow-up questions during the interview call. Refrain from asking them; instead, take notes. If you decide to ask the person to come in for an interview, you can use those questions to guide your discussion.

In some cases, a candidate will want to ask you questions as well. Be sure to maintain control of the conversation and not allow the applicant to interview you. If the candidate wants to know about your management style or your sales culture, for example, restate that the call is intended only as a preliminary conversation. For example, you could say, "I appreciate the questions you're raising. If we do get to a face-to-face interview, I'd welcome the opportunity to have that conversation with you then."

If you find yourself talking to someone who's really interesting or engaging, it can be tempting to extend the conversation beyond 15 minutes. However, you want to save a longer interaction for a face-to-face meeting, when you'll be able to glean more details about body language and presentation. Don't make the mistake of thinking you've found the perfect person for the job in a single phone interview. You never know how the hiring process will evolve, so stick to your process and make efficient use of your time.

Here are some other tips to keep in mind as you're conducting phone interviews:

- **Listen carefully.** If you speak too much, you won't get enough information about the person to screen the candidate effectively.

- **Assess how articulate and persuasive the candidate is.** You're hiring for a sales position, so you should look for someone who presents well on the phone.

- **Say one or two positive things about the position and why you believe it's an appealing opportunity.** Many good candidates have multiple options, so you want to take a moment to build interest. However, don't spend an undue amount of time talking about how great the job is. Remember, the main purpose of the phone call is to understand more about the candidate.

In-Person Interviews

The in-person (or "in-depth") interview is your chance to get a deeper impression about the candidate and ask questions to find out if he or she fits the attributes of your job profile. Unfortunately, many managers make the mistake of asking leading questions in an interview. For example, you might say, "We're really a team-oriented culture. Are you a team player?" This is obviously a leading question. Almost anyone would know enough to respond by saying, "Yes, I'm a great team player!" You're left with no genuine insight and aren't well equipped to make a good selection.

The most effective questions are behavior based. They help you uncover how the candidate aligns with the attributes you're looking for (per your job profile) by focusing your questioning on specific behaviors aligned with those attributes. Take the attribute of resilience as an example. Here are some behavioral questions that would help you uncover a person's resilience.

- "Tell me about a problem you encountered that was particularly difficult to overcome."
- "Describe what you were doing when this problem or obstacle occurred."
- "How did you combat this challenge?"

- "What was the outcome?

- How will this situation affect your outlook when similar problems arise?"

The more detailed the response the candidate gives, the more likely the accuracy. In an interview, you're hoping to get the most accurate portrait possible before you extend an offer to a candidate; and that's exactly why behavior-based interviewing works so well.

Industry Experience or "Best Athlete"

Many sales managers debate whether it's best to hire someone with industry experience, or a "best athlete" (someone with limited industry experience who has exceptional selling skills).

It's an interesting dilemma. Someone with industry experience likely comes equipped with product and service knowledge, a stable of valuable contacts, and a well-honed approach to dealing with buyer personalities. On the other hand, someone with industry experience can also be very set in his or her ways. And those contacts might not be so valuable upon close examination because they may prefer to continue to do business with the salesperson's previous employer.

A best athlete, on the other hand, has attributes that align well with your job profile and will likely perform well in any environment. We generally advocate hiring a best athlete since research tends to indicate that people who are good at selling can pretty much learn to sell anything well. That said, there are some scenarios where it makes sense to take industry experience into serious consideration.

- The learning curve (regarding product features or knowing how to sell to high-level decision makers) is steep and you believe it will take too long for a new hire to ramp-up without industry experience.

- You sell in an industry with a small, tight-knit network of buyers and your candidate has existing relationships with those potential buyers.

If either of these points are true for your organization, you'll likely want to at least consider hiring with industry experience in mind. Generally speaking, however, the person who best matches your job profile should be your primary candidate.

Selecting the Right Candidate

At this point, you should have narrowed down your candidates to no more than two people who you can present to your manager and/or Human Resources team. These candidates should align with the attributes of your job profile, and you should feel confident about extending an offer to either one of them. **The Candidate Selection Tool (Appendix A)** will help you narrow your choice to the best two candidates.

It might seem like an obvious point, but never send a candidate to your boss who you wouldn't want to join your sales team.

Ideally, someone from the Human Resources team should conduct reference checks—simply because there are so many legal considerations surrounding the issue of talking to former employers. Finally, when you're ready to extend an offer, keep the following in mind:

- Make the offer as quickly as possible once you've made a decision. Popular candidates are in high demand.

- Give the candidate a deadline for responding. (Provide a reasonable length of time.)

- Let the candidate know how excited you would

be to have him or her join your team and reinforce why you believe this is a great opportunity.

Key Hiring Takeaways

- Creating the Job Profile: Make sure to include the skills and personal qualities (e.g., motivation, work ethic, integrity) that are essential for success.

- Sourcing Candidates: Always focus on building your candidate pool, even when you don't have a job opening.

- Interviewing: Use behavior-based questions to determine if candidates possess the personal qualities you've identified.

- Selecting the Right Candidate: Use the Candidate Selection Tool to help you evaluate and compare candidates.

Section 3

Managing Your Team

Everyday sales managers make dozens of decisions and work through a seemingly endless to-do list. In this regard, learning to focus and prioritize management functions is invaluable.

Behavior-Based Performance Management

The one element common to all sales managers, regardless of specific responsibilities, is that their primary role is to achieve results *through and with* others. This is a classic definition of management and forms the foundation of what sales managers do on a daily basis.

So what does this mean in practice? Research consistently shows that to achieve peak performance from your sales team a sales manager needs to:

1. **Communicate performance expectations** so each individual knows what is expected of him or her and how success will be measured.

2. **Monitor and manage behaviors** so each individual knows what behaviors will lead to success.

3. **Monitor results** on a regular basis so that corrective action and / or positive reinforcement happen in a timely manner.

4. Provide regular feedback to assist with ongoing professional development and sharing of best practices.

The heart of this process is managing behaviors. Behaviors are the observable actions a salesperson uses to achieve results—e.g., the salesperson made 20 prospecting calls per day this week. We monitor and manage behaviors because positive and consistent behaviors lead to positive and consistent results. You can't manage or improve results unless you manage and improve behaviors.

To some people, it may be a provocative idea to put your primary focus on behaviors. Aren't results all that matter? What many managers don't understand is that the best way to get great results is to monitor and manage behaviors. This will help you proactively address performance issues that impact results.

Results have already happened; they are backward looking. The only way to impact future results is to focus on behaviors that lead to the desired results. Our experience is that sales managers spend too much time reviewing results (backward looking) and fail to monitor and manage the behaviors (forward looking) that lead to results.

A critical first step in implementing a behavior-based performance management system is to carefully think about the key results you need to monitor, and then determine what behaviors will drive those results. You can think of "results" as the outcomes of behaviors. For example, you might help the salesperson set a goal to acquire a certain number of new customers within a given time frame. If the goal is to acquire four new customers before the end of the quarter, you want to help the salesperson define the behaviors that will produce that outcome or result.

The following desired results would be driven by the associated behaviors.

Desired Result: New Customer Acquisition

Behaviors:

- Develop a territory plan, including a comprehensive list of prospects.

- Create account plans that map the key decision makers and influencers.

- Set first-time meetings with prospects.

- Add new opportunities to the sales pipeline.

Desired Result: Sell More to Existing Customers

Behaviors:

- Develop an account penetration strategy.

- Get referrals to new decision makers and influencers from existing contacts.

- Schedule meetings with new decision makers and influencers to identify their needs.

- Develop and present solutions that are responsive to their needs.

As a manager, you want to monitor behaviors so you can help the salesperson make adjustments in time to achieve great results. Most importantly, make sure to provide ongoing feedback. When the salesperson completes one of the behaviors you've agreed upon (e.g., "set 10 first-time appointments this week"), provide acknowledgement and encouragement. By the same token, step in and proactively discuss any behaviors that aren't being completed (e.g., "I thought you were going to submit your account plans last Friday and I haven't seen them yet").

It's important to limit the number of key results you want to monitor; focusing on too many results may require an exponential (and overwhelming) number of behaviors. For example, if you decide to monitor 10 results, this could potentially lead to as many as 40 behaviors (assuming four behaviors tie to each result). Realistically, you should manage no more than eight to 12 behaviors for each salesperson. That means you should focus on two or three results. You should also make sure to specify the time frame for completion.

Communicating Expectations

When these results and corresponding behaviors have been identified, you can turn your attention to communicating clear expectations regarding results and behaviors.

While often overlooked, communicating expectations is vital. Does your sales team really understand what you want them to do (behaviors) and what you want them to achieve (results)?

Sales managers often use vague language (either in meetings or emails) when describing performance expectations. They then mistakenly assume that salespeople clearly understand what's expected of them.

For example, a manager may send an email that says, "We are tracking behind this quarter and need to take our game to the next level." Unfortunately, this statement is close to meaningless. At most, a salesperson will understand that results are not as good as they need to be and that he or she needs to sell more. While this may be true, it lacks clarity and purpose. Additionally, it doesn't address what specific behaviors are expected from each individual salesperson.

To avoid this type of confusion, you should make sure you clearly set expectations by adhering to the following communication guidelines:

1. Personalize the communication and make sure it is realistic. The communication should be specific to the salesperson you are speaking with, and not a general message.

2. State the desired result(s). Make sure your communication includes what you want the salesperson to achieve.

3. Include the behaviors required to produce these results. These are the specific actions that, if performed well, should lead to the desired result.

4. Define metrics for assessment, including the time frame. It should be clear how you will measure performance and over what period of time.

5. Check for understanding. Ask the salesperson to recap his or her understanding of your expectations.

Let's imagine the result you want is for the salesperson to achieve $350,000 in sales for the quarter. Here's an example of how you could verbally communicate this expectation using the elements listed above.

"To achieve $350,000 in Q4, you will need to close an additional $127,000 by the end of the quarter (December 31). In order to accomplish this, I would like you to conduct in-person meetings with at least five of the seven customers that are in the "proposal" stage of your sales pipeline by next Friday (December 12).

Given your history of success with customers (70 percent close rate for opportunities in proposal stage), this should allow you to exceed your target number if you can get these meetings scheduled by next Friday. Please let me know if this makes sense to you and what steps you will take following this discussion."

[Pause, listen to response, and check for understanding.]

"Great. Let's plan to reconnect next Monday (December 8) to review where you stand on appointments, discuss the specific goals for each meeting, and how I can help."

Managing Performance Gains and Gaps

Feedback is a powerful performance management tool. All too often, however, sales managers:

- Focus only on what the salesperson is failing to do (performance gaps) and forget to point out what the salesperson is doing right (performance gains).

- Wait far too long before providing feedback about performance gaps.

Performance Gains

Why is it important to reinforce performance gains? This type of feedback is a great way to motivate and empower salespeople. Also, articulating performance gains makes it easier for salespeople to both understand and repeat the behaviors that are helping them achieve great results.

Effective feedback is specific. Such comments as "great quarter" or "good job this week" ring hollow. Instead, clearly connect your feedback to 1) behaviors and 2) results. This way, the salesperson will understand what he or she is doing right. A more meaningful statement to a salesperson that just beat his or her quota is, "Great job this quarter! Not only did you exceed quota, but by executing on your target plan you also brought in seven new accounts, which bodes well for future quarters. Nice way to set yourself up for success."

Performance Gaps

One of the reasons you must monitor behaviors and results is so you can identify performance gaps early on. Some managers neglect pointing out performance gaps until they are "forced" to conduct annual performance reviews. As a result, they live with subpar performance far longer than necessary.

As soon as you spot these signals, your first step is to make sure you've set clear expectations. How can you tell? Look for patterns. Is this performance gap prevalent across your team, or isolated to that individual salesperson? If multiple salespeople are having the same issue, it's probably worth examining expectations that were set (i.e., whether they were clearly communicated and reasonable).

To ensure that your communications are both clear and reasonable, make sure you always include:

- Desired results: What you expect them to accomplish.
- Desired behaviors: What they will need to do to achieve the result.

- Define metrics: How you intend to measure the result.

- Timeframe: When you expect them to achieve the desired result.

- Reasonableness: Have other salespeople achieved similar results in similar situations?

Next, you want to act quickly. Always provide feedback sooner rather than later; and never assume performance gaps will improve on their own. (It's very rare for managers to look back and say they should have waited longer before addressing performance gaps.)

Assuming the basis for the performance gap rests with the salesperson, engage in an open, supportive discussion to determine the underlying causes. As a starting point, share what you've observed—and over what period of time. Then, make sure to provide an opportunity for the salesperson to respond to ensure there is agreement on the performance gap. If there's any disagreement or misunderstanding, clearly restate the expectations (verbally and in writing) and set up a meeting to review the salesperson's progress.

Assuming there is agreement on the performance gap, determine (with the salesperson's input) whether this gap is due to a lack of motivation and/or due to a deficiency in skills/knowledge. This is essential because the management actions required will depend on these factors.

Taking Action

Unfortunately, when it comes to taking action, managers often feel like their options are limited to living with the status quo, putting the salesperson on a performance plan, or terminating the salesperson. In reality you have a much broader set of options, including coaching, training, counseling, and discipline. Most important, keep in mind that you are actually helping support the salesperson's development when you are proactive in reinforcing performance gains and addressing performance gaps.

The Sales Performance Checklist

The following checklist illustrates how you can efficiently address performance issues on your team.

- ✓ Does the salesperson know expectations? It can be surprising how many performance problems stem from salespeople not knowing what specific behaviors and results are expected of them.

- ✓ Are the expectations being met? If the salesperson is meeting expectations, you should provide positive reinforcement and then delegate as much responsibility as possible. This is how you most efficiently leverage your time and effort to produce exceptional sales results.

✓ Does the salesperson know how to meet expectations? Use training and/or coaching to resolve skills or knowledge gaps. As a best practice, plan to spend 25 to 40 percent of your time coaching and developing your team.

✓ Does the salesperson make proper effort? Sometimes the performance problem is not caused by a skill or knowledge gap but rather by the salesperson's poor attitude or low motivation. Here the appropriate management action is to counsel the salesperson and address the attitude or motivational problem.

✓ Does the salesperson receive appropriate rewards and consequences? You can be an enabler of poor performance by poorly structuring compensation plans (that incentivize the wrong behaviors) or by not taking a firm (but fair) approach to performance improvement plans.

✓ Do obstacles block performance? The salesperson may not have the resources to be successful, or the sales goals may be unrealistic. In these cases you need to provide more resources, remove the obstacles, or reassess your expectations.

If the salesperson is still underperforming after going through this process, it is appropriate to work with Human Resources to either reassign this person to a role where he or she is likely to be successful or terminate him or her from the position.

For a handy reference guide on managing performance gaps and gains, refer to the **Sales Performance Causes/ Action Flowchart (Appendix B)**

Performance Counseling

Sometimes a performance problem is due to factors other than lack of skill or knowledge. That's where performance counseling comes in.

Performance counseling is designed to address motivation or attitude problems. Such problems require a different approach to feedback. Typical signs of motivation or attitude problems include the following:

- Decrease in productivity.

- Excessive complaining (about insufficient leads, for example).

- Disrupting other people's work.

- Bad-mouthing other employees, the company, or management.

Performance Counseling: Your Role and Mindset

If the performance problem is related to attitude or motivation you should consider performance counseling. Your role in performance counseling is to identify problems and bring them to the attention of the salesperson by explaining how his or her behavior is negatively affecting performance or other people. In other words, discuss with the salesperson the observable negative impact of the behavior.

Once you've identified the problem, address it directly. That is, establish guidelines for the salesperson to improve the situation. There can be a very fine line here between solving problems and improving performance—particularly when job performance is negatively affected by the salesperson's personal problems.

Your role is not to solve employees' personal problems or act as a therapist. Your role is to work with the employee to find methods to improve performance. Having said this, you should be aware of certain situations you should not deal with alone (for example a violation of company policies, medical illness, mental-health disorders) that might affect a salesperson's work performance. These situations should be reviewed with your Human Resources department before you discuss them directly with the salesperson, even if you only suspect these problems are present.

Like all management actions, performance counseling works best when you protect the self-esteem and confidence of the salesperson. Remember to:

- Focus counseling on behaviors.

- Avoid attacking or labeling people in negative ways.

- Focus on plans for improvement, not on excuses or blame.

- Be sure guidelines for improvement are practical and likely to produce positive results.

- Show and demonstrate that you care about the success of your sales team and their efforts to succeed.

Much of what makes managers effective comes as a natural expression of care: you are involved, supportive, positive, and always treat people with respect. In return, you'll earn the respect and trust of your team.

How to Lead Performance Counseling Session

Sales managers often feel uncomfortable conducting a performance counseling discussion. Having a clear process is critical to ensuring that the performance counseling session is productive and focused.

Step 1: Open the Session in a Positive and Serious Way

This is critical because performance counseling can sometimes be awkward for you and the other person, so you want to get the performance counseling discussion off to a positive yet serious start.

You should begin by mentioning positive past performance, if you think it's appropriate. This kind of positive reinforcement—especially if it's directly related to the performance problem at hand—reminds the employee that he or she can do the job, and that you recognize his or her capabilities.

You could say, "I recognize that you are capable of meeting these expectations, because you've done so in the past."

You should also state the purpose of the session, which is to help the salesperson improve the behaviors that are negatively impacting his or her job performance.

You then want to quickly transition to the specific problematic behavior and review related performance expectations. Here you want to pinpoint the indicators of a performance problem. These include any observable actions, words, or behaviors (for example, excessive lateness or absence, a decline in productivity, or an increase in customer complaints) that you think require performance counseling.

Step 2: After You've Opened the Session, Wait for a Response

Give the salesperson a chance to react. It is not uncommon at the beginning of a performance counseling session for a salesperson to deny that anything is "wrong." In other cases, the salesperson may offer reasons or excuses for the problematic behavior or results.

Step 3: Seek and/or Offer a Solution

Your primary objective should be to get the salesperson to develop a solution. The performance counseling session should be a conversation, not a lecture. Ask questions. For example, you could say, "What do you think you can do differently to improve in this area?" Prepare your questions beforehand so you know how to guide the discussion.

One of your most important questions in almost any performance counseling session will be, "What will you do to change and improve your behaviors?" If the salesperson offers vague or unworkable solutions, state why you have concerns that their approach will not work and offer your own solutions.

Step 4: Gain Commitment to the Proposed Solutions

Once you've discussed the solution(s) with your salesperson, you should confirm that he or she is in agreement and willing to take the steps necessary to address the underlying performance issue. If you're unable to gain his or her agreement, you should politely conclude the performance counseling session, and consult with Human Resources on next steps.

Step 5: Establish a Method to Follow Up

Schedule a one-on-one follow-up meeting for a specific date, location, and time. The purpose of this session is to review progress relative to the plan you've outlined, discuss any obstacles, and brainstorm solutions. In some cases (depending on the scope of the plan), you may need a series of follow-up meetings.

Step 6: Close the Session in a Positive Manner

Stress your belief that the salesperson can improve. Reinforce positive behaviors and the opportunity to improve.

Step 7: Document Your Performance Counseling Session

It's always wise to check with your Human Resources team in advance to review the situation, get their input, and determine what type of documentation they might need regarding performance counseling. This documentation may be important down the road if you decide to put the salesperson on a formal performance improvement plan or to terminate his or her employment.

Key Sales Management Takeaways

- Behavior-Based Performance Management: Focus on monitoring and managing the sales behaviors that drive results.

- Communicating Expectations: Make sure you include the desired result, the specific behaviors required, and the timeframe for completion.

- Managing Performance Gaps: Assess the underlying cause(s) to determine what action(s) you should take.

- Performance Counseling: Focus on a proactive, respectful plan to improve performance.

Managing the Sales Pipeline

Managing the sales pipeline is a critical aspect of managing team performance. If you were promoted from the field, you probably already know that the sales pipeline holds information about pending sales opportunities, and consists of various stages relating to the advancement of those opportunities. However, the salesperson's relationship to the pipeline is materially different from that of a manager.

For the manager, the pipeline has two primary functions. First, it's a coaching tool. The information in the pipeline will provide structure and focus for the weekly discussions you'll have with salespeople. The aim of these discussions is to develop strategies that help salespeople advance their sales opportunities and close more deals.

Second, the pipeline is now a reporting tool. You'll use pipeline metrics to create sales forecasts, which get handed off to upper-level managers and executives so they can see how much revenue the sales team is expected to bring in for the month or quarter. You should always be mindful that the executive team wants to see 1) an accurate forecast, and 2) higher win rates.

Salespeople have a much different relationship with the sales pipeline. For one thing, they are eternal optimists—no matter how long a deal has been lingering in their sales pipeline, they believe that a "yes" is just around the corner. Your average salesperson also believes that his or her manager will respond more positively to a full pipeline (even if it is full of dormant opportunities). Compounding this problem is the tendency of salespeople to avoid labeling stalled opportunities as "inactive" because they perceive that it will be a poor reflection on their selling skills.

Avoiding a Bloated Pipeline

Twenty years ago or more, it was far easier to avoid a bloated sales pipeline. That's because managers and salespeople typically tracked opportunities on a white board. Since space was limited, the sales funnel on the white board was reserved for active opportunities. This sales funnel was then used as the basis for weekly reviews with each salesperson. The manager would ask a series of questions:

1. "What sales calls did you go on last week, either with new or existing clients?"

2. "What are the key action items from each call?"

3. "Are there any new opportunities we should add to the sales funnel based on these meetings?"

4. "How about existing opportunities? What do you see as next steps with each opportunity?"

Frequently, the manager and salesperson would discover that some opportunities had stalled. Without a strategy to reengage or advance the opportunity, the opportunity would be taken out of the pipeline; however, the salesperson would keep that prospect on his or her radar as a an opportunity to reengage or pursue in the future. This practice helped keep the pipeline from becoming cluttered with deals that weren't likely to close that month or quarter.

This discipline is often missing in an age where pipelines are managed in CRM systems with unlimited storage capacity. Salespeople are asked to enter every new opportunity into their CRM system in order to share information across the sales organization, and then to advance the opportunity through various pipeline stages until it is either "won" or "lost." Although CRM systems substantially increase pipeline visibility (a good thing), they can also quickly become a wasteland for older, inactive, "stuck," and—in many cases—unqualified opportunities.

Over time, the pipeline becomes bloated with opportunities that are in different stages for widely disparate time periods. Since this information is readily available and tracked by senior sales leaders, they want to know which opportunities are realistic, how soon those deals might close, and why such a high percentage of opportunities seem to be "stuck."

This is certainly not a criticism of CRM systems, but it does help explain the mandate for better pipeline management.

The Relationship between Sales Process and Pipeline

Why do upper-level executives want accurate forecasts? They use the projections contained in the sales forecast to make countless decisions—from production capacity, to hiring decisions, to investment decisions. Other than gut feel and past experience, most sales managers don't have a defined process for how they arrive at these numbers, or an explanation as to why they think their current forecast will be more accurate than the forecast from last month or quarter.

When sales teams use CRM systems to manage the sales pipeline, they typically match the progression of a deal to the stages of their sales process. While there is nothing fundamentally wrong with converting your sales process into pipeline stages, it is essential that the criteria associated with each stage (i.e., the things that need to occur before an opportunity advances to the next stage) are driven by customer actions. In other words, the customer actions, not the salesperson's activities, need to trigger advancement through the sales pipeline.

For example, it is a lot more meaningful for a design firm to have "customer signs off on a prototype" as a criteria to advancing to the next stage in its sales pipeline rather than "prototype has been submitted to the customer for approval." Although both actions are necessary, only the customer's actions move the opportunity forward through the sales pipeline.

Three Steps to Improve Forecast Accuracy

Given these challenges, here is a process you can use to help your sales team better manage opportunities and eliminate "bloat" from the sales pipeline.

Step 1: Develop Objective Criteria

A critical first step in avoiding a bloated pipeline is developing objective criteria for each stage of deal progression. Before an opportunity can advance from one stage to the next, it must meet certain criteria. As an example, before an opportunity can leave the "needs discovery" stage, the following criteria must be satisfied:

The customer …

- has acknowledged a business need.
- understands economic consequences of solving problem.
- has identified a budget to address the problem.
- has agreed to a solution presentation on a specific date.

We have worked with many sales teams where the criteria were fuzzy or, worse, non-existent. In those cases, salespeople and their managers moved opportunities through the pipeline based on subjective judgments. Not surprisingly, without objective criteria in place to check the salesperson's natural enthusiasm, these teams had bloated sales pipelines with a significant number of opportunities languishing in the earlier stages of the pipeline.

By including objective criteria for each stage, you can review and confirm the opportunity has actually met the criteria. You can also apply more consistency to how various salespeople categorize their respective opportunities. This ensures a cleaner, more accurate, pipeline.

Step 2: Assign Reasonable Probabilities

Each stage in the pipeline should include a probability factor based on an analysis of prior wins and losses. Going back to our example above, you may use historical data to reasonably assign a 25 percent probability of closing for opportunities in the "needs discovery" stage.

CRM systems typically pre-assign probabilities based on the sales stage. These pre-assigned probabilities may be very different from your actual experience and, as a result, will lead to inaccurate forecasts. Carefully consider whether these default values are accurate and whether each opportunity "deserves" to be classified at that stage based on your objective criteria. Remember, explaining how your team beat projections is a far more appealing task than explaining why you came up short.

In pipeline review meetings, ask the salesperson to predict not only when the deal will close, but also when the customer will take the next set of actions required to advance the opportunity. This "next action date" can be critical to determining when a deal is stuck. When the salesperson fails to get commitments from the customer based on the established criteria, then you should adjust the close date and/or decrease the probability factor.

During a pipeline review, salespeople frequently get very uncomfortable "committing" to a specific sales forecast. Why? Because they intuitively know that many of the deals in the pipeline won't close by the date they entered into the CRM system, or they have numerous deals they know are dead but they haven't wanted to remove them from their pipeline until they are able to replace them with new opportunities.

One suggestion to better manage the pipeline is to create a contest that rewards the salesperson who come closest to the number he or she forecasted at the beginning of the month or quarter. By getting a commitment to the forecast and reviewing it at the end of the month or quarter, you can increase the level of visibility and attention from your salespeople and reinforce the importance of managing the sales pipeline.

Step 3: Track Velocity

The velocity of a sales pipeline is the speed at which the opportunity is advancing through the sales pipeline. The key considerations here are the overall amount of time an opportunity has been in the sales pipeline, and, even more important, how long the opportunity has been in the most recent sales stage. One of the most effective ways to avoid a bloated pipeline is to specify how many days an opportunity can remain in a particular stage before the status is changed to "inactive." By taking this approach, inactive opportunities are managed separately and do not inflate the sales forecast, which should be solely based on active opportunities.

As an example, in a business where the sales cycle averages six months, it might make sense to assign opportunities that have been stuck in a particular stage for 60 days to the "inactive" stage. Inactive opportunities can then be reviewed separately and not factored into the sales forecast until they meet the criteria to advance to the next stage.

By assigning objective criteria and reasonable probabilities to each pipeline stage and eliminating inactive opportunities, you will rationalize the sales pipeline and create consistency across the sales team; this will result in better, more accurate, sales forecasts.

Key Pipeline Management Takeaways

- Avoiding a Bloated Pipeline: More opportunities do not equate to a better pipeline. More "active" opportunities is the goal.

- Objective Criteria: Develop objective criteria for each stage of the pipeline based on customer-driven actions.

- Sales Forecasts: Assign reasonable probabilities to each stage of the pipeline. It is better to err on the conservative side and make sure your forecast is only based on "active" opportunities.

- Track Velocity: Determine a reasonable time period for each stage of the pipeline based on your sales cycle. Opportunities that exceed the allotted time should be designated as "inactive" until they progress to the next stage.

Coaching Your Team

We all have images and ideas from the sports world about what it means to be a great coach. But what we see on the surface is only a fraction of the type of work and dedication it takes to become a successful coach. Coaching is not just about shouting advice from the sidelines or giving inspiring locker-room speeches. Great coaching starts with the right mindset.

Sales Coaching Mindset

The big mental shift that sales managers must make is that the primary goal of coaching is helping others succeed. That means the mark of your success as a coach is measured and recognized by their achievement —not your own performance.

Sales coaching is about helping, supporting, monitoring, and facilitating. It's not about telling salespeople what to do. If you get salespeople invested in coaching outcomes, they're more likely to take initiative to change their behavior and see results. In this way, a collaborative mindset transfers the "heavy lifting" of changing behaviors from the coach to the person being coached. This allows you to scale your efforts across an entire team, which raises the bar for performance.

Almost all salespeople are grateful for having a manager who's also a great coach. Selling can be a tough job, and there's rarely one right answer. When salespeople encounter roadblocks, advice from an experienced and supportive sales manager is invaluable. Not only can you help keep deals from getting stuck or lost, you can also help salespeople advance opportunities through the pipeline by developing their skills and knowledge. As you help multiple salespeople reap these benefits, the level of performance is raised for the whole team. That's the power of great sales coaching.

If you want to succeed as a sales coach, adapt your plan to reflect each salesperson's specific needs. It is the highly customized nature of coaching that makes it uniquely effective at developing high-achieving salespeople. No off-the-shelf sales training program can meet the specific development needs of each individual member of your team in the same way as sales coaching.

The Three A's Framework

Collaboration is the heart of sales coaching. When salespeople are invested in coaching outcomes, they're much better able to achieve and sustain behavior change.

To achieve this objective, base your sales coaching conversations on the Three A's Framework.

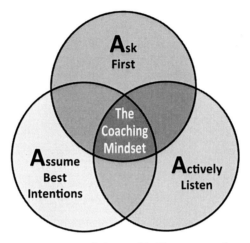

Figure 5.1: Three A's Framework

1. *Ask First*

The purpose of asking questions is to promote self-discovery by the salesperson. Salespeople will take more ownership of changing their behavior if they feel they are discovering problems and solutions on their own. To achieve this outcome, ask open-ended questions and allow ample opportunity for salespeople to reflect and respond. By asking questions, you will also gain a better sense for their perspective which, when it comes to coaching, may be more valuable than your own.

2. *Actively Listen*

Listening is essential to a collaborative sales coaching mindset. Unfortunately, many sales managers are poor listeners—they feel like they need to do all the talking to get their point across. By contrast, most successful sales coaches excel at "active listening," which means they are fully focused on the salesperson.

Concentrate on what the salesperson is saying, and tune in to such nonverbal communication signals as tone of voice and body language. Don't simply wait for your turn to speak; listen with the intent to understand what the other person is saying.

When you do respond, continue to follow the principles of active listening by asking questions to clarify meaning and confirm understanding—and paraphrasing what the salesperson has just said in order to communicate your understanding to the salesperson.

3. *Assume Best Intentions*

The tone of sales coaching conversations should be congenial and open-minded, not punitive or retaliatory. Assume your salespeople want to improve their skills; this assumption helps create a positive environment in which salespeople feel comfortable acknowledging shortcomings and are motivated to improve. Remember, part of their growth involves allowing them to make mistakes. Resist the temptation to pass judgment before you understand their intent.

Two Types of Coaching

Great sales coaches are proficient at both opportunity coaching and skills coaching. Opportunity coaching is typically short-term oriented and focuses on helping your salespeople advance and close specific opportunities in their sales pipeline. Skills coaching is long-term oriented and focuses on helping salespeople improve their selling skills and techniques.

Opportunity Coaching

The aim of opportunity coaching is to help salespeople close more business. This is different from the sort of pipeline cleansing that happens during a pipeline review meeting. Opportunity coaching is designed to provide salespeople with actionable and (if necessary) intensive assistance. There are all sorts of reasons salespeople might need this kind of help. Consider the following examples:

- The prospect suddenly experiences a budget freeze.

- A new competitor has emerged.

- Access to decision makers is denied.

- A new decision maker is introduced into the deal.

- A competitor is offering a lower price.

The goal of the opportunity coaching session is to identify where the salesperson has more work to do in terms of research, planning, identifying customer needs, or crafting the solution. If there are too many gaps and the salesperson can't answer key questions, the discussion may need to focus on whether the opportunity is actually qualified or, at a minimum, whether it should reside in an earlier pipeline stage.

You can constructively coach opportunities by asking five questions.

1. "What is the customer's business need?"

A key to a successful sale is solving a customer's business problem or improving a customer's existing situation in a way that is compelling. Can the salesperson succinctly characterize what the customer is trying to accomplish with this initiative and how it will impact business? If not, he or she often misses the opportunity to really understand the business need and make a connection to how his or her solution addresses the need. If the salesperson is simply responding to an inbound lead or RFP, he or she might not be able to articulate the prospect's business need and explain how your company's solution solves the customer's problem.

Coaching Point: Help the salesperson develop questions to ask the customer to more clearly understand the business need.

2. "What is the unique value you bring?"

Once the need is identified, can the salesperson clearly articulate the unique value his or her solution provides? Can he or she explain why his or her solution is different and how it will benefit the organization in unique ways? Again, if salespeople can't explain it quickly and simply, he or she probably has more work to do.

Coaching Point: Help the salesperson develop and practice a value proposition that explains the unique aspects of your offering and how it brings value to the customer. A good value proposition 1) restates the customer's need, 2) conveys the value of your solution, 3) differentiates you from the competition, and 4) includes some form of third party proof.

3. *"Who are the decision makers, and what is your relationship with them?"*

Salespeople often get trapped selling too low in the organization, with no clear picture of who will make the ultimate purchase decision or how it will be made. Suddenly a "mystery decision maker" shows up who has a preference for the competition and the deal is lost. The goal is to identify and gain access to the real decision maker(s) as early in the process as possible. Leveraging the salesperson's network within the account can help him or her identify the true decision maker and potentially gain an introduction.

Coaching Point: Help the salesperson create a plan to identify and access other stakeholders in the organization who may be able to influence the decision and provide access to the decision maker(s).

4. *"How will the competition try to beat you?"*

It's not enough to know who your competitors are; you must also know their strengths and weaknesses and how they compare to your company and your offering. It's fair to ask the prospect who else he or she is talking to and how many vendors might be on the short list. If you get an answer (and you may not), this information can be invaluable in helping you develop a proposal that leverages your unique strengths relative to your competition.

Coaching Point: Help the salesperson develop a matrix of strengths and weaknesses for your solution compared to the competition to identify key messages you want to present to your customer.

5. *"Why will you win?"*

Finally, you must help your salespeople develop compelling reasons why your solution is superior to other options the customer is considering, including the customer's potential decision to not purchase any solution (i.e., "do nothing"). These are not generic differentiators, but specific, tangible reasons that show why and how the customer would receive the most value from your solution. If your salesperson can't articulate why your company's solution best addresses the customer's needs, he or she is not positioned well to win against the competition. Your salespeople need to believe in their competitive points of differentiation and convince you that they have presented the best option to the customer.

Coaching Point: Work with the salesperson to identify and write down two or three reasons your solution is absolutely the best option for the customer. Make sure the salesperson has complete faith in those reasons.

Skills Coaching

Skills coaching focuses on helping your salespeople develop more effective selling skills. Skills coaching should take place on a regular basis with all of your salespeople to help them improve in numerous areas, including:

- Prospecting.
- Building relationships.
- Call planning.
- Identifying needs.
- Presenting value.
- Managing objections.
- Negotiating.
- Closing.

Knowing When to Coach

Because sales coaching is so effective, it's easy to fall into the trap of thinking it can solve any problem. Unfortunately, that's not the case. In fact, repeated attempts to coach chronically weak performers might simply be an inefficient use of your time.

Great sales coaches understand where coaching is most effective, and they spend the majority of their time trying to make good salespeople better. The Development Matrix is a useful tool to help you figure out when to coach and when to pursue other management options.

To use this matrix, start by conducting a selling skills assessment of your salesperson. When assessing selling skills, think in terms of "proficiency" (the salesperson's skill level) and "motivation" (the salesperson's desire to apply the skill).

In figure 5.2 (Development Matrix), we have included an example where a sales manager has assessed a sales person on eight key selling skills.

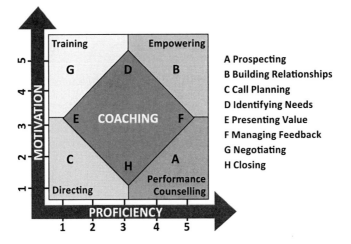

Figure 5.2: Development Matrix

By plotting your assessment of the salesperson's skills on the Development Matrix, you'll quickly determine when coaching will be most effective. Listed below are various management actions (including coaching) you should take based on your skills assessment of the salesperson.

Empowering

Assume you have a salesperson on your team who's great at building relationships and rates extremely high in both proficiency and motivation. In this case, you want to increase this salesperson's control and accountability; therefore, empowerment would be the most effective management action. For example, you can empower by expanding the salesperson's authority to manage a large account without your direct involvement. When you allow a highly skilled and motivated salesperson to take on more responsibility, not only do you empower that person, but you also free up your own time.

Training

When a salesperson isn't proficient in a certain skill but is highly motivated, training (not coaching) is the best initial action. Typically, new salespeople are good candidates for training. In our example (see figure 5.2), training would be an appropriate management action for improving this salesperson's negotiating skills. However, note that reinforcement of the skill through coaching is a key component of helping salespeople retain and apply their newly learned skills.

Directing

When a specific skill rates low in both proficiency and motivation, you need to direct, not coach. That means providing specific instructions on how, what, and when to accomplish a task. As a manager, there are many times when it is appropriate to direct, including when a salesperson is new to his or her position. In our example (see figure 5.2), the salesperson needs to be directed to do better call planning (not an uncommon occurrence). That said, having to continually direct a salesperson is a very inefficient use of your time; and if too many skills fall into this area, you may need to reassess whether this person is a good fit for this position.

Performance Counseling

Performance Counseling is appropriate when the salesperson has previously demonstrated high proficiency in a certain skill, but—for whatever reason—now has low motivation. One common skill area in which we see this is prospecting. Some salespeople may be good at prospecting but, after a few years on the job, suffer from burnout, so their motivation can be low. Performance Counseling focuses on attitude and motivation.

Coaching

Because coaching assumes a baseline level of proficiency, the "Coaching Diamond" is the largest area on the Development Matrix. Simply put, most salespeople have average proficiency and motivation for a majority of their skills. So it is likely that the most common management action you use to develop your team's skills will be coaching.

In figure 5.2, notice how the majority of the skills (Identifying Needs, Presenting Value, Managing Feedback, and Closing) are best addressed through coaching. The reason coaching is so powerful is that, as skills go from "average" to "high," they move to the Empowerment quadrant. Again, if you can empower more salespeople, you'll get the benefits of 1) better performance from them, and 2) more time for yourself to pursue other management activities.

Co-Assessment

Before meeting with a salesperson to discuss coaching, it's important that you assess their skills and determine which management actions will be most effective.

Your next step is to ask the salesperson to assess his or her own skills using the same assessment tool. The purpose of having the salesperson self-assess is to secure the salesperson's buy-in for your coaching sessions.

We often find that sales managers have an aversion to co-defining coaching outcomes and prefer to just tell the salesperson to fix the problem. Remember, however, that one of the essential qualities of coaching is collaboration. When the salesperson believes he or she is contributing to the coaching process, the salesperson will be more receptive to input and will take more responsibility for changing behaviors.

You might also gain important insight by comparing perspectives. For example, you may rate a salesperson low in a particular skill but, based on the salesperson's input, conclude that legitimate outside factors are the root cause of the problem. This would open up valuable and constructive dialogue. In other cases, you may uncover that certain skills are more pressing based on the input you receive from your salesperson.

Once you have buy-in from the salesperson on what to coach, you should then work together to develop a **Sales Coaching Plan (Appendix C)** for improving future performance. As part of the Sales Coaching Plan, you and the salesperson should identify specific opportunities where you can observe the salesperson on a coaching call.

Three Types of Calls

As a sales manager, there are three types of sales calls that you can go on with a salesperson: coaching call, joint call, and modeling call.

Coaching Call

As previously mentioned, skills coaching is best done by observing your salespeople in action, and then discussing strengths and development areas together. That means accompanying them on coaching calls.

The purpose of the coaching call is for you to observe the salesperson and gain insight into how he or she is using selling skills. This means the salesperson—not the manager—does the selling.

Bear in mind that, sometimes, the best coaching happens after a salesperson makes a mistake. In the short run, this can be painful to watch, but, in the long run, this is highly beneficial for salespeople in developing their skills.

Modeling Call

The objective of a modeling call is for the salesperson to observe while the manager sells. This allows the manager to demonstrate the skill and show proper execution. A modeling call is most appropriate for a new salesperson who is still building experience and confidence, or for a salesperson who has a persistent development need in a certain area.

Joint Call

Joint calls involve very little coaching. On a joint sales call, a sales manager's role is to help the salesperson sell. Perhaps the salesperson has specifically asked for help with an account, or maybe the opportunity is so significant that you want to accompany the salesperson on the call. Remember, the primary goal of a joint sales call is to close business. Accordingly, it's entirely appropriate for you to actively participate during the sales call.

You should only go on a limited number of joint sales calls (as opposed to coaching calls). If you find yourself going on too many joint calls, you are doing the salesperson's job. Remember that your primary job is not to sell—it's to manage your salespeople and help improve performance across the entire team.

Keep in mind that while each of these types of calls has its purpose, the coaching call is your best option for helping your salespeople develop selling skills.

Five-Step Process for Sales Coaching

A consistent coaching process is essential to provide effective coaching. Figure 5.3 illustrates a five-step sales coaching model that provides a consistent, replicable coaching process.

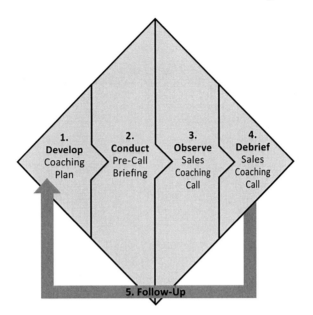

Figure 5.3: 5-Step Sales Coaching Model

1. Plan Coaching Visit

All coaching calls should be conducted with very specific objectives in mind. You should begin by identifying two or three selling skills you want to coach the salesperson on during the next few months. Although there may be numerous other areas for improvement, these are best deferred until the initial skills have met expectations. Please see **Coaching Call Observation Form (Appendix D).**

When working with the salesperson to identify sales calls, be sure to choose situations that will likely offer good opportunities for you to observe the specific skills you've agreed on. For example, if you're working on the skill of managing customer objections, select a sales call with a customer who's further along in the buying process and might raise objections.

You should then review the sales coaching objectives with the salesperson and discuss what specific skills you be evaluating on upcoming sales calls.

2. Conduct Pre-Call Briefing

A pre-call briefing lasts about 10 to 15 minutes and takes place before each sales call. A pre-call briefing should begin with the salesperson describing the account history and status. Next, discuss the salesperson's objectives for the sales call. Then review the coaching focus by discussing specific skills he or she should be demonstrating during the sales call.

You should also discuss the respective roles you'll each play during the call to avoid any confusion. Again, the best coaching occurs when you observe and the salesperson sells.

3. Observe Sales Coaching Call

When observing a sales call, let the salesperson take the lead, and focus on the objectives you both established during the pre-call briefing. When you meet with the customer, let the salesperson make introductions. If possible, sit to the side so the primary interaction is between the customer and the salesperson. If the customer addresses questions to you, it is best to respond briefly and then tactfully redirect him or her to the salesperson.

That said, there are some cases where it's appropriate to "rescue" a salesperson during a coaching call. This must be intentional, however, and not a knee-jerk reaction. Here's a list of questions to consider when deciding whether or not to rescue the salesperson.

- Is the salesperson in danger of jeopardizing the sale or account relationship unless I step in?
- Will rescuing the salesperson seriously damage the salesperson's credibility?
- Will my participation enhance or impair the salesperson's development (including their confidence/attitude)?
- Is the salesperson saying something that goes against company policy?

If none of the above circumstances apply, it is usually best to remain in observation mode. Remember, your goal is to build a better sales team through effective coaching, not to demonstrate your personal expertise during a sales call. Instead of stepping in, make notes about specific situations you want to review later with the salesperson.

4. Debrief Sales Coaching Call

After a sales call, debrief as soon as possible—potentially, even on the car ride to the next call.

Resist the temptation to immediately share what went wrong or what the salesperson could have done better. Instead it is best to open with a positive comment on an aspect of the call that went well. You should then ask the salesperson for their perspective both on what went well and areas for improvement. Remember, you should express your opinion only after you have a full understanding of the salesperson's perspective. Even if you eventually have to advocate your position, you'll be more persuasive if you begin the coaching conversation by asking questions and letting the salesperson speak first.

Here's a questioning sequence you can use to guide your debriefing session.

Observation questions: "What …

… surprised you about the customer's reaction?"

… did you notice when you started asking the customer more questions?"

Reflection questions: "So, what …

… went well?"

… could have been better?"

Application questions: "Now, what …

… would you do differently?"

… steps will you take?"

After you've heard the salesperson's perspective, you will have valuable insight to share. At this point, be concise and provide actionable advice. You should also be prepared to support your recommendations with examples. If the salesperson has really missed the mark, try suggesting a different approach. To gain the salesperson's commitment to try a new approach, use the following tips:

- Cite success others have had applying the skill or technique.

- Describe situations where you have seen great improvements using the particular skill or technique.

- Ask how he or she will apply skills in the future.

- Offer your support.

When providing feedback, focus on the salesperson's behaviors, not judgments about those behaviors. A judgment is not helpful to the salesperson unless it's followed with a specific description of behaviors. If you say, "You did a great job on that call," there is no specific information about what was great. A better way to say this could be: "You did an excellent job by clarifying the client's objection by asking, 'Are you concerned about the delivery schedule or implementation?' before answering the customer's concern." This statement tells the salesperson he or she did a good job and describes the behavior upon which the judgment was made.

At the end of the debrief, summarize the salesperson's performance and work together to develop an action plan for improving future performance. The salesperson should practice his or her new knowledge and skills as soon as possible. Practice can take the form of an informal role play, another sales call, or an assignment that requires the salesperson to learn and practice a specific skill.

5. Follow Up

The final step of coaching is follow-up. Your role here is to monitor the salesperson as he or she practices and develops new skills, and to determine when the skill has been mastered.

Consistent follow-up has the following benefits:

- Reinforces and helps solidify new skills and behaviors.

- Holds the salesperson accountable for using his or her new skills.

- Demonstrates your commitment to the salesperson's growth and development.

- Sustains behavior change.

You should establish a positive tone at the beginning of follow-up meetings by summarizing the salesperson's strengths. Ask questions and have the salesperson share ideas and opinions about his or her development efforts. Probe for what results he or she is experiencing as the salesperson tries out the new skills. Acknowledge that skills and new behaviors require some time and energy to master.

Follow-up should also include encouraging salespeople to share their successes with their peers during your sales meetings. The salesperson can briefly describe the skills he or she is working on and describe how the application of these skills has yielded good results. This can potentially motivate others on your team to improve their skills as well.

In advance of each calendar quarter, work with your salesperson to formally evaluate his or her progress and update the coaching plan accordingly. If certain skills have been mastered, it's now time to work on other skills that will have a positive impact on future performance. Part of your follow-up should include reaching agreement on future development needs. Make sure you both agree on the two or three skills most important for your salesperson's ongoing development.

Managing Resistance to Coaching

Sometimes salespeople get defensive when you provide feedback. They may deny they have a development need or try to deflect the blame for performance challenges. Some of these quotes may sound familiar.

- "That's not how we did things at [previous employer]…"
- "I don't know what you're talking about. That meeting went well."

- "The real problem is that I'm not getting good leads."

It can be very frustrating when salespeople don't want to be coached, but it's important not to match resistance by using a more forceful tone. This will create conflict and won't help you achieve your ultimate sales coaching goal of modifying the salesperson's selling behaviors.

Here are some guidelines to manage resistance.

Consider the Salesperson's Perspective

One fundamental mistake sales managers make when providing coaching feedback is not adequately considering the salesperson's perspective. It may be that the salesperson's resistance to your coaching is based on an underlying substantive issue.

For example, you may want the salesperson to prospect for new business using a script developed by the marketing team. The salesperson, on the other hand, believes the script sounds contrived and feels uncomfortable using it. Perhaps the salesperson is raising a legitimate point. Rather than argue, work with the salesperson to edit the script, put it into his or her own voice and maintain the key points marketing wants to communicate.

Another consideration is to pick your battles carefully. If the salesperson in our prospecting example is booking a sufficient number of appointments using his or her own approach, it may not be worth the effort to try to get him or her to change the behavior.

Investigate the Underlying Issue

Let's assume the salesperson is booking a sufficient number of appointments, but the quality of these appointments is low. You've observed that this salesperson is "badgering" prospects into agreeing to appointments, rather than creating genuine interest.

In this case, you need to address the salesperson's behavior by investigating the issue and addressing the source of it, without creating more hostility.

Tactics to Manage Resistance

Here are some effective tactics:

- **Boomerang.** Here you turn the issue back on the salesperson. The boomerang tactic helps make the coaching more collaborative as you ask the salesperson for his or her input. ("That's a great point. Do you have any ideas about that?")

- **Refocus.** When a salesperson tries to deflect your coaching feedback, refocus the conversation. ("You raise a good point about the quality of leads. While this is worth exploring with marketing, let's focus on the steps you can take to improve your prospecting skills and techniques.")

- **Defer.** Sometimes dealing with issues as they come up may sidetrack the coaching process, so it may be better to defer these issues. ("I understand your concern about lead quality. Let's talk about leads at our weekly one-on-one meeting.")

Provide Direction

If the salesperson still resists your coaching efforts, you should consider escalating your intervention and directing. Many sales managers confuse directing with barking out orders—e.g., "Do it my way!" However, it's much more effective to provide salespeople with specific and clear directions as to what you want them to do differently and your rationale. Here are six steps to follow.

1. **Describe the specific behavior you observed.** You say: "I noticed on a series of sales calls that, when customers raise objections, you tend to directly address the objection and skip the step of acknowledging and clarifying the objection to

make sure you fully understand what the customer is objecting to."

2. **Identify the pitfalls and impact of the behavior.** You say: "By skipping this step, you may fail to communicate empathy, and you risk not fully understanding the nature of the objection itself."

3. **Reinforce the behavior you want to see.** You say: "What I'd like to see you do differently is use the managing objections model we covered in our training. First, you acknowledge the objection to show empathy. Then, you clarify the objection to make sure you fully understand it. You address the objection based on your understanding and, finally, confirm that your response meets the customer's expectations."

4. **Explain the reasons for your directive.** You say: "Following this model will help you develop a better relationship with the customer. Ultimately this approach is far more collaborative and is likely to help you build a stronger rapport."

5. **Check for understanding.** You ask: "Does this approach make sense to you?"

6. **Talk about next steps.** You say: "Great! I'd like to see you use this approach over the next few weeks whenever you encounter an objection. Let's meet

again in about a month to discuss how it's working for you."

Employ Other Management Actions

Sometimes, even directing doesn't work. Maybe your salesperson has the requisite skills to prospect effectively, but lacks the motivation. In these cases, you should consider employing other management actions. These could include performance counseling, revised performance expectations, or even assigning the salesperson to a different role.

Sales coaching should never be a struggle between you and the salesperson, and coaching won't work if the salesperson feels threatened. A great sales coach creates a safe coaching zone where the salesperson perceives it is okay to make mistakes (and that the coaching is not a backdoor performance review). Focus on behaviors, avoid making judgments, and tailor your approach based on each of your salesperson's specific development needs.

Are You a Good Coach?

A formal self-assessment of your coaching abilities will shed light on how you rate in some of the key skill areas for coaching a sales team. But beware—your perspective may differ from that of your salespeople.

If you want a more insightful assessment of your coaching effectiveness, consider having your team assess you anonymously, and then compare the results. This may be a real eye opener.

If you don't have access to a formal self-assessment or don't want to go through the process of having your own team assess you, you can use a very simple self-assessment. Ask yourself: "Would I want to be coached by me?" For this self-assessment to work, you must be brutally honest. Here are some other questions to consider.

- Do your team members ask you to join them on sales calls (not to sell, but to be coached)?

- Reflect on how you respond to selling "mistakes." Do you see them as learning lessons?

- Do salespeople seem to feel demoralized or disheartened at the end of a coaching call?

- Have you set the salesperson up for success by practicing before the call?

- Do you follow up with the salesperson and continue to provide encouragement?

By answering these questions honestly, you can gain insights into how effective of a coach you are and identify areas for your own improvement.

While the assessments described above measure coaching-related behaviors, the rate at which your sales team's skills improve is a true reflection of how effective you are. Document the skills and behaviors you're trying to help salespeople improve, and then track your results. This may sound like a lot of work, but it's ultimately the only measurable way to know if your coaching is making a difference.

For example, imagine you have a salesperson on your team who performs well until it comes to closing. When she encounters resistance, she wraps up the sales call rather than probing to uncover the objection. As a result, she loses the sale.

In this scenario, "probing to uncover the objection" is the behavior you want to coach and track. Practice the skill with her before the sales call, observe her during the call, and give her feedback after the call. If you can see improvement in the way she asks questions and uncovers objections over the course of her next five sales calls, you've had a significant impact.

Key Sales Coaching Takeaways

- Sales Coaching Mindset: Avoid telling. Coaching is best supported by the 3 A's Framework (<u>A</u>sk First, <u>A</u>ctively Listen, and <u>A</u>ssume the Best of Intentions).

- Opportunity Coaching: Leverage your experience to help your salespeople develop specific actions to advance or expand sales opportunities.

- Skills Coaching: Coaching is most effective when it's limited to two or three skill areas.

- Coaching Call: Your role as a coach during a coaching call is to observe, not to sell.

- Debriefing: Resist the temptation to start with what went wrong. Always begin with a positive comment (what went right) and then use questioning to have the salesperson analyze the call.

Leading Your Team

Developing and Achieving Your Sales Vision

The best sales managers demonstrate great leadership and know how to motivate and inspire their teams. One of the key ways to become a sales leader is to create a vision for sales success. This vision will help your team focus on their goals, prioritize their activities, and stay motivated even when they encounter obstacles. It's what separates high-performance teams from those that simply drift or fail to evolve beyond achieving short-term goals.

A sales vision is a statement that indicates where you want your sales team to be at some future time. Figure 6.1 illustrates the five-step process to create and achieve the goals that will make your vision a reality.

Figure 6.1: Sales Vision Pyramid

1. Create Your Sales Vision

First, you must decide what you want to achieve. That could be in regard to sales within your company or relative to your competitors. For example, your sales vision could be to be one of the top three districts in the company within the next 12 months. Here are some characteristics of a good sales vision.

- A sales vision must be challenging. It must be something above and beyond average goals and expectations.

- A sales vision should take anywhere between six and 18 months to achieve. Any vision that can be reached in fewer than six months is typically too narrow to be a true vision. Conversely, a vision that requires 18 months or more is probably too far-reaching.

- A sales vision should be attainable. That is, it must be realistic enough to be achievable if you and your team stretch a bit.

- Your sales vision should also specify some positive change that you are committed to realize through a concerted effort with your sales team.

2. Translate Your Sales Vision into Goals

The next step in developing a sales vision is to establish goals that align with your vision. The more specific your goal, the easier it will be to communicate them to the team and the easier it will be for the team to understand, commit, and work towards them. Think of the goal as a key milestone you will need to achieve on the path to realizing your vision.

Make your goals SMART: Specific, Measurable, Attainable, Relevant, and Time-bound. So, if your sales vision is to be one of the top three districts in the company within the next 12 months, a related SMART goal could be to increase sales volume by 15 percent by June 30.

3. Develop Strategies

The next step is to develop strategies. Strategies describe how you will achieve the goals. For instance, in pursuit of your goal to increase sales volume by 15 percent by June 30, you could increase your team's sales coverage by hiring additional salespeople, running a special sales incentive program for the sales team, or targeting key accounts to grow existing business. Each of these strategies directly ties back to the goal.

4. Identify Tactics

Now that you've created your vision, established goals, and developed strategies, you must now identify specific action steps, or tactics. In other words, what steps need to be taken, by whom, and by when? Keep these tips in mind when identifying your tactics.

- Identify major activities or benchmarks. Just as you would note landmarks on a road map, you should identify key points and activities in your action plan to stay on the right track.

- Clearly define roles and responsibilities. Each team member should have a specific role in carrying out tactics and helping achieve goals that track to the sales vision. As part of this exercise, identify where you might need help from other departments or teams, and include those colleagues in your action plan. For example, if you're focusing on a new product offering, you might need to contact marketing and ask them to develop supporting sales collateral.

- Specify target dates for completion. In order to move closer to your goal and reach it within the designated timeframe, set target dates for each action step. For example, if your strategy for increasing sales is to broaden coverage by hiring more salespeople, a supporting tactic could be to work with Human Resources to source and interview at least three qualified candidates within the next 30 days.

5. Communicate Your Vision

It's not enough to simply create and document the sales vision—it won't be successful unless it's communicated and discussed with the team. Great leaders have a clear vision regarding where they want their team to be at some future time—and they communicate it every chance they get. Your clarity, commitment, and passion to achieve the vision is what guides and keeps the team on track.

Communicating your vision is essential to build and maintain momentum. An effective communication strategy covers all levels of the organization. Using many different methods to communicate will help ensure the message is received and understood. Sales meetings, individual discussions, coaching sessions, emails, and telephone calls should consistently reflect your leadership and commitment to achieving the vision.

Please see **VisiPlan Tool (Appendix E)** to create your sales vision for your team.

How to Make Important Decisions

As a sales manager, you'll have to make important decisions on a daily basis, including decisions about performance issues, resource allocation, customer challenges, and new sales opportunities.

Your ability to influence your team is directly related to how well you make decisions. To become a better decision maker, use the following process.

Step 1: Weigh the Importance of the Decision

Ask yourself how important the decision is. How much time, money, and energy should you spend on making the decision based on the decision's relative importance? For instance, you may not want to put too much time and effort deciding on a date and time for your next sales team meeting, but you'd put considerable effort into figuring out the best way to roll out a price increase to your customers.

Step 2: Search for Relevant Facts and Information

Although this sounds obvious and simple, it's an easy step to skip since most sales managers prefer to make decisions quickly. However, when you make quick decisions, you sometimes overlook important information. Once you acknowledge missing facts, you must determine if they're worth finding and if you have the time to invest in searching for them. Ask yourself the following questions in searching out relevant facts/information.

- What are the criteria for this decision?
- What information do I need?
- Are the missing facts worth finding?
- How much time do I have?

The most effective decisions are made with as much information as the decision requires. The answers to the questions above will determine when you should accelerate your decision making.

For example, let's say you've just learned that a key account intends to pull its business in a few days. In this situation, you probably lack the time necessary to proceed methodically. It may take too long to analyze call reports or schedule a strategy session with upper management to see what you can do to retain the business. This would be a case where you should act quickly, even though your information isn't comprehensive.

Step 3: Identify Your Options

Develop a list of options and the associated actions if you were to pursue each option. Focus on the obvious possibilities first, and then include some less obvious, more creative ideas. Then, narrow your list down to two or three of the most viable options.

Step 4: Use a Risk / Opportunity / Investment Framework to Compare Options

Now you are ready to compare your most viable options in terms of Risk, Opportunity, and Investment using high, medium, and low rankings.

- **Risk:** How likely is it that you will get your desired result with each option?

- **Opportunity:** What impact will each option likely have on results? In addition to how well it will solve a problem, consider how your decision will affect other issues, such as sales performance, your team, and your credibility.

- **Investment:** How much will it cost to implement each option? Besides the financial cost involved, each option will require a high, medium, or low degree of your time, the sales team's time, and other resources.

One common decision-making bias leaders have is downplaying the non-monetary (hidden) costs of decisions that otherwise look like low-risk, high-opportunity decisions. These hidden costs can include longer-than-expected ramp-up time of new hires, lost productivity implementing new systems or processes, or time out of the field attending in-person meetings.

Step 5: Select the Best Option

The last step is to select the best option based on your Risk, Opportunity, and Investment rankings. Listed below are four criteria to help you identify the best option.

- **Eliminate Low-Opportunity Options:** These options will seldom be your best options, so eliminate them right from the start.

- **Eliminate High-Risk / Low-Probability Options:** A risky decision is one that could impact your credibility as a leader with your team. To increase the likelihood of success, eliminate options that are high risk and have a low probability of success.

- **Weigh High-Investment Options:** Be sure to calculate the direct and indirect costs associated with each option.

- **Select the Option Closest to the Ideal:** Ideal = Low risk, High opportunity, and Low investment.

Remember, there will always be some tension between these factors and the goal is to achieve the right balance in terms of risk, opportunity, and investment.

After selecting the best option, communicate your decision to your sales team quickly. Why is timing essential? If you've followed a systematic decision-making process, revisiting a decision after it has been made (assuming no new information has surfaced) won't improve the quality of the original decision. On the contrary, a delay risks losing a valuable opportunity or letting an existing problem worsen. Moreover, unnecessary delay can frustrate your team and damage their faith in your leadership abilities.

How to Influence Your Team

Great leaders understand how to influence the thoughts, actions, and behaviors of the sales team. This influence is critical to provide your team with clear leadership and motivate salespeople to achieve your vision.

Depending on the salesperson and the situation, you should consider using different styles. The challenge is to select the most appropriate style for each situation.

There are four distinct sales management styles: directing, persuading, participating, and delegating.

1. Directing

Directing is mostly one-way communication. In these situations, you tell the salesperson what you want him or her to do. Although directing has a negative connotation, it is appropriate and effective in specific situations. Directing requires confidence in the information you are providing and specificity in delivering it.

Use a directing style:

- To communicate decisions.
- To provide instructions.
- At impasses.
- To communicate policies and procedures.

2. Persuading

Use this style when you want to convince your sales team to move in a particular direction. In this scenario, you attempt to gain commitment by convincing others that what you're saying is accurate or is the best option.

Use a persuading style to:

- Introduce a new or different selling technique.

- Present a new concept, idea, method, or procedure.

- Exceed already-established sales goals.

- Challenge the sales team.

3. Participating

Participating is used to get input, buy-in, feedback, or opinions from the sales team. The participating style encourages two-way communication and an open, honest exchange of ideas. You have an opportunity to access a variety of ideas and to show that you respect and value the input of your sales team.

Use a participating style to:

- Get a salesperson's perspective on problems.

- Obtain suggestions for improving individual performance.

- Gather information on the progress with an account.

- Brainstorm strategies for further development.

4. Delegating

Delegating empowers salespeople with the freedom to do their jobs or to enhance their personal development. Salespeople who have demonstrated the ability to work successfully and independently often have the confidence to continue to perform with little supervision.

Use a delegating style:

- With successful salespeople who have demonstrated abilities and expressed a desire to work independently.

- To develop individuals by building their confidence in their own ability to work successfully with little supervision.

Although each sales leadership style is distinct, you will find that many situations require more than one style. For example, in a sales meeting you may need to use the persuading style to introduce a new sales strategy, and follow that with the participating style to get ideas on how to implement the strategy. No matter what the situation, remain flexible and use the different approaches as needed.

The more flexible you are in the use of management styles, the greater your ability to communicate and influence behavior in the desired direction.

Six Common Motives of Salespeople

We all have different motives that drive us and those motives and their intensity can change over time. For example, a salesperson may be specially driven in the early stages of a sales contest when their expectations of winning are high. As the contest progresses, their drive may diminish if they feel that they are too far behind to win.

Salespeople tend to be driven by one or more of the following six Motives: Money, Opportunity, Teamwork, Independence, Visibility, and Excellence.

1. Money

This is the most obvious motivator. Money, or what money can buy, is important to most salespeople. However, it isn't necessarily most important to everyone. Other motivators may be equally or more important. Ways to impact and/or support money as a motivator include:

- Relating sales results to financial gain or reward.
- Adding incentives for higher performance.
- Discussing and reinforcing financial goals.

2. Opportunity

Many salespeople are driven by opportunity. Motivational opportunities usually fall into the categories of challenges and the possibility of improving one's situation.

When you've recognized this motivation in members of your sales team, you should try to create an environment that offers opportunities. Ways to create and foster opportunities include:

- Showing how success can lead to advancement.
- Providing for career opportunities where possible.
- Delegating responsibilities that prepare the person for promotion.

3. Teamwork

Many salespeople enjoy being part of a team and are motivated by the idea of contributing to the success of the group. They derive satisfaction from solving problems as part of a group, contributing to a co-worker's success, or even playing a major role at a sales meeting. If you identify teamwork as a motivating factor for a salesperson, you should:

- Get the salesperson involved in team projects.
- Build team-based goals and incentives.
- Provide team recognition.

4. Independence

While some salespeople are motivated by teamwork, many salespeople prefer to work independently. This involves empowerment, independence, freedom, and enhanced feelings of power and control. This motivator should not be ignored or minimized simply because people belong to a team. For any salesperson motivated by independence, you can:

- Delegate special projects or assignments.
- Provide greater autonomy and accountability.
- Reinforce their success at working independently.

5. Visibility

Recognition, approval, or a need to stand out from the crowd drives some salespeople. When a salesperson is motivated by visibility, you should:

- Highlight successes with a personal note, team recognition, or recognition from upper management.

- Be sure the salesperson knows his or her accomplishments are appreciated and recognized.

- Allow the salesperson to share his or her accomplishments in a group setting.

6. Excellence

Most salespeople want to perform well. The difference between the "excellence" and "opportunity" motivators is that the excellence-motivated person wants to excel at what he or she does and is not necessarily seeking higher and more challenging goals and opportunities. Excellence means the person takes great pride in achieving or surpassing personal and professional expectations.

When a salesperson is motivated by excellence you should:

- Recognize the achievement of goals.

- Acknowledge consistency of good results.

- Reinforce the benefits of his or her high quality work.

The best way to understand what drives your salespeople is to observe their behaviors and ask them what they enjoy most about their job. By taking the time to observe how they work and understand their perspective, you will gain incredible insight into their key motives.

Confidence in Your Team

If you're convinced your salespeople are all capable of achieving their goals and you let them know it, this will reinforce their desires and motivation. Consequently, they will very likely achieve (and perhaps surpass) goals. On the other hand, if you doubt they can do it, they'll pick up on that sentiment. This, in turn, could lower your sales team's self-confidence and prevent salespeople from performing well.

Here are a few suggestions to keep things moving in a positive direction.

- Co-develop goals and associated action plans to enhance the salesperson's confidence.

- Acknowledge and reinforce each salesperson's respective strengths.

- Recognize achievements and progress toward goals.

Key Sales Leadership Takeaways

- Sales Vision: Communicating a vision keeps your team focused and engaged.

- Achieving Your Vision: Determine the underlying goals, strategies, and tactics required for success. A vision that does not include these elements is not likely to be achieved.

- Decision Making: How you make and communicate decisions impacts your credibility as a leader.

- Influence and Motivation: How you persuade and motivate others depends on the situation and requires flexibility.

Transforming Into a High-Impact Sales Leader

Throughout this book we have touched on the fundamental aspects of becoming a High-Impact Sales Manager. These include developing the skills and techniques to 1) recruit and hire the right people, 2) manage sales performance, 3) manage the sales pipeline, 4) coach and develop your team, and 5) lead and motivate your team. These areas not only provide the foundation for sales management success, but are also the building blocks for your career growth and advancement.

As such, this final section is focused on how you can continue to grow and develop as a sales leader. Unlike the other skills defined in this book, these attributes are subjective and driven by your actions and attitude. They are an overall perception of characteristics, traits, and personality, which makes up a positive image of you as a sales leader—someone your salespeople will eagerly follow because they trust you and have confidence in your decisions. Because personal abilities are largely based on your behavioral characteristics, they are hard to measure and equally hard to change and develop.

Recognition of your development needs is the first step. Think about this by considering the following leadership traits and assess yourself based on your sales team's perspective (i.e., their perception of you as their leader).

I…

- Am a good role model.

- Am enthusiastic and optimistic.

- Have a sincere and honest personality.

- Have integrity and follow through on my commitments.

- Have earned my team's confidence, trust, and respect.

- Demonstrate empathy when appropriate.

- Maintain a positive, action-oriented philosophy, even in the face of challenges.

- Respond quickly when salespeople have questions or problems.

The more of these traits that apply to you, the further along you are in developing your leadership abilities.

Ultimately, everyone has room for growth in each of these areas, and there are times where you may fall short. Therefore, think in terms of "growth" as opposed to "achievement" when examining your traits. As a High-Impact Sales Manager, you'll realize that personal growth and career growth are inextricably linked. Accordingly, we encourage you to strive for improvement as part of a long, successful, and rewarding career.

Appendices

Appendix A: Candidate Selection Tool

Use this guide to compare candidates and make the best selection.

Rate each candidate: 10=highest; 5= medium; 1=lowest on a scale of 1–10:

	Cand. 1	Cand. 2	Cand. 3	Cand. 4
Job Profile Factors:				
Education				
Work experience				
Performance				
Personal qualities				
How Well Will Each Candidate:				
Prospect for new business				
Build rapport				
Plan for sales calls				
Identify buyer needs				
Present value				
Manage customer feedback				
Negotiate based on value				
Close deals				
Manage customer relationships				
Totals				

Appendix B: Sales Performance Causes/Action Flowchart

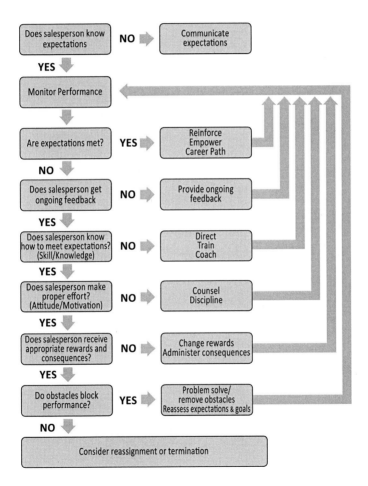

Does salesperson know expectations **NO** ➡ Communicate expectations

YES ⬇

Monitor Performance ⬅

⬇

Are expectations met? **YES** ➡ Reinforce Empower Career Path

NO ⬇

Does salesperson get ongoing feedback **NO** ➡ Provide ongoing feedback

YES ⬇

Does salesperson know how to meet expectations? (Skill/Knowledge) **NO** ➡ Direct Train Coach

YES ⬇

Does salesperson make proper effort? (Attitude/Motivation) **NO** ➡ Counsel Discipline

YES ⬇

Does salesperson receive appropriate rewards and consequences? **NO** ➡ Change rewards Administer consequences

YES ⬇

Do obstacles block performance? **YES** ➡ Problem solve/ remove obstacles Reassess expectations & goals

NO ⬇

Consider reassignment or termination

Appendix C: Sales Coaching Plan

For: _____

From _____ to _____

Top 3 Coaching Priorities
1.
2.
3.
Areas to Investigate:

Date	Skills to Coach	Coaching Calls	Follow-Up

Appendix D: Coaching Call Observation Form

Salesperson: _____ Date: _____

Account/Contact: _____

Background: _____

Call Objective: _____

1. Coaching objectives for this call:

Skills	Behaviors to Observe

Areas to investigate: _____

2. Coaching observations:

Behaviors	Examples of When Used Well/Not Well

Other observations: _____

_____

New coaching priorities: _____

_____

Follow-up/Next steps: _____

_____

Appendix E: VisiPlan Tool

Date: _____

VISION (*Where* do you want to be?)

GOALS (*What* will you need to achieve to get there? Make the goals SMART: specific, measurable, action-oriented, realistic, time-bound)

STRATEGIES (*How* will you achieve your goals? What is your overall approach?)

TACTICS (For each strategy, *what actions* need to be taken, by whom, and by when?) Use a separate Tactical Action Plan form for each strategy.

Tactical Action Plan		
Strategy (from VisiPlan):		
Action Steps	Who	Target Date

Glossary

Behaviors: The specific actions one takes or things one does in pursuit of goals. Behaviors drive sales performance/results.

Best Athlete: A salesperson who has attributes that align well with your job profile and will likely perform well in any environment.

Feedback: Your input, as a management and coaching tool, to improve sales performance.

Goals: What you want to achieve.

Joint Sales Call: A type of sales call where the manager's role is to help the salesperson sell.

Judgments: An assessment or evaluation that expresses an opinion.

Modeling Sales Call: A type of sales call where the manager's role is to sell while the salesperson observes to learn proper technique.

Opportunities: Potential sales deals in the pipeline.

Opportunity Coaching: Sales coaching designed to help salespeople advance sales opportunities.

Options: A list all of the possible decisions a sales manager could make.

Performance Counseling: Counseling designed to address a salesperson's attitude or level of motivation.

Performance Gains: Performance that exceeds expectations.

Performance Gaps: Performance that falls short of expectations.

Personal Qualities: Attributes sales managers should look for when evaluating potential candidates for hire.

Pipeline Velocity: The speed at which the opportunity is advancing through the sales pipeline.

Pre-Call Briefing: A 10-15 minute meeting between a sales manager and salesperson prior to a sales call.

Results: What you have achieved; typically driven through the performance of behaviors.

Sales Pipeline: A tool used to track sales opportunities (typically included within a CRM system).

Sales Training: A program that helps salespeople learn, apply, and adopt new selling skills and techniques.

Sales Vision: A statement that indicates where the sales manager wants his or her sales team to be at some future time (typically six to 18 months out).

Selling Skills: The specific techniques that can be used to increase sales effectiveness.

Skills Coaching: Coaching that focuses on the development of selling skills.

"Star Athlete" Syndrome: The ill-fated notion that a top salesperson will automatically become a highly effective sales manager.

Norman Behar

Norman Behar is a proven sales leader with over 25 years of CEO and senior sales management experience. He is recognized as a thought leader in the sales training industry, and has worked with clients in a wide range of industries including financial services, healthcare, technology, manufacturing, and distribution. Norman's white papers and blog posts are frequently featured in leading trade publications. Previously, Norman served as President and CEO of Catapult, Inc., a leading provider of personal computer training services, where he oversaw operations and managed growth prior to the company's acquisition by IBM. Norman received his B.A. from the Foster School of Business at the University of Washington, where he graduated Summa Cum Laude.

David Jacoby

 David Jacoby has extensive experience developing and implementing innovative sales training and sales leadership development solutions for clients. David is a thought leader in instructional design and the use of innovative technologies to deliver industry leading online sales training programs. Previously, David has served as Vice President of Business Affairs of Xylo, Inc., where he was responsible for the Company's sales operations, legal affairs and financing activities. Before joining Xylo, David was a corporate attorney with Skadden, Arps, Slate, Meagher & Flom LLP, where he practiced in the firm's mergers & acquisitions group. David received his J.D. from the Columbia University School of Law, where he was a Harlan Fiske Stone Scholar, and received his B.A. from the University of Washington, where he graduated Summa Cum Laude.

Ray Makela

 Ray Makela has over 25 years of management, consulting, and sales experience. As a Managing Director at Sales Readiness Group, Ray currently oversees all client engagements. Previously, Ray served as Chief Customer Officer (CCO) at Codesic Consulting, where he was responsible for business development, managing customer relationships, and the development and implementation of Codesic's sales-training initiatives. Ray has also held management positions at Accenture and Claremont Technology Group where he was a management consultant in the Change Management practice. Prior to his consulting career, Ray served as a Division Officer and NROTC Instructor in the US Navy. Ray earned his B.A in Speech Communications from the University of Washington and an M.P.A. in Public Administration and Information Systems Management from the University of Southern California.

About Sales Readiness Group

Sales Readiness Group (SRG) is an industry leading sales training company that helps businesses develop highly effective sales organizations. SRG solutions include comprehensive sales training, sales coaching, and sales management programs that deliver sustainable skills improvement.

SRG sales training programs are customized to meet its clients' specific requirements. SRG training programs include:

- Industry leading training content.

- Customized case studies, examples and exercises.

- Pre and post training assessment.

- Experienced, engaging facilitation team.

- Comprehensive reinforcement programs.

- Integrated technologies to promote skills adoption.

To learn more about how SRG can help you improve sales performance, visit www.salesreadinessgroup.com